Creative Writing for Adult Learners

Improve your writing skills & learn to express yourself

Amanda J Harrington

author of A Crash Course in Creative Writing & the Creative Writing for Kids series

GW00728039

Contents

Introduction

For anyone needing help to improve their writing skills or inspiration on how to express themselves, How To books can seem either too simplistic or too intense. This book is designed to be fun and challenging, offering a real boost to your creativity while giving you lots of practice in writing techniques.

The exercises in this book have been used by job hunters, adults taking entrance exams or functional skills tests and adult learners who have left English behind at school and want to enjoy creative writing.

Some exercises are more complex than others, but guidance is given throughout. For the first two parts of the book, there are also examples with every exercise, showing you how they can be done.

This book is intended as a guide for those who have not been used to expressing themselves creatively or who want to return to creative writing after a break. It can be completed on its own, or as well as the other books offered for adult creative writing by Amanda J Harrington.

A beginning

The very first thing I want you to do is write a short
piece about yourself. Imagine you are introducing and
describing yourself. Include details of how you look,
your age, your lifestyle, what you like to do and anything
you think other people might be interested in.

Don't worry about getting this right, it's just a warm-up
exercise. Make sure to keep this piece of writing though,
as we'll need it later.

Creative Writing in Letters

You are going to write some letters. We'll start with familiar letters and then move on to ones which are more imaginative. Don't worry if you struggle to think of something to write; if this happens, just move on to the next letter. You can always come back and complete exercises at another time.

Letter 1: A short note

Write a note to your friend to let them know you're going to be late getting home. Tell them three things you think they should know. Keep it short and chatty.

Here is my note:

Hi, really sorry but am going to be late (again!). Let yourself in and put the kettle on. There are biccies in the cupboard next to the fridge. Please make sure the cat stays in.

Letter 2: Thank you...

Remember when you were little and had to write thank you notes? Well, here we go again! Write a thank you note to your elderly aunt who has sent you a truly horrendous set of hand-knitted socks, gloves and ear-warmers. Be nice but try to include a little bit of honesty too.

Here is my thank you note:

Thank you for your very thoughtful present. I'm so glad I won't be cold this winter. It was very kind of you to include the ear-warmers as you know I suffer from earache. I hadn't expected that shade of purple but it means I won't lose them in the house, so it was a good choice.

Letter 3: Uncle Arthur

Uncle Arthur has been stuck in his bed for three weeks and is getting very fed up. Write him an upbeat, friendly letter to take his mind off things. Include a mention of his car and tell him when you can visit.

Here is my letter:

We've been busy at this end, getting ready for our visitors. We've had to redecorate the spare room and we found Jennifer's old roller blades - you remember, the ones she lost when she was six. Amazing what turns up when you're not expecting it.

Sorry to hear the little car hasn't been well but at least it will be ready to drive again once you're both back on the road!

I've got a present for the car as I know you won't want me to bring presents for you. I'm not telling you what it is. All I'll say is that Jennifer chose it so I hope the car likes it - I'm not sure you will!

We'll be through to see you this Sunday and hope you're feeling better by then.

Letter 4: Complaining

Now something a bit less friendly. You are going to write a letter of complaint to the manager of a business you have used lately. This could be anything, like a restaurant, garage, museum, local shop, dry cleaners - anything where a service has fallen short of what you expect.

Be as descriptive as possible about what went wrong. Don't be nasty or rude but do try to get your point across. This doesn't have to be a long letter, just one full of words that paint a picture for your reader.

Here is my complaint:

I have been coming to your café for years and have never had a visit like the one last Friday. Your waitress, Yvonne, was obviously in a bad mood and I had to send my wife to bring her to take our order. She had a bad attitude at the table and glared at me when I asked her to repeat herself.

She was untidy, her hair wasn't fastened up properly and there was a dirty smudge on her cheek. When I asked her if she had remembered to wash her face, she was very sullen and rubbed the stain off with the back of her sleeve.

When she took our order, she turned and flounced away, leaving us in no doubt about how she felt. She talked to the other waitress and pointed across at us too. I don't appreciate being made fun of when I have come to spend my money, especially not from people who should know better.

I believe I am a patient and polite person, but I see no reason to put up with bad behaviour. Your waitress should be able to put a happy face on for everyone who comes into the café - after all, we pay her wages! In future, I will say more than I did to Yvonne and will leave her in no doubt about how I feel.

Do you see how you can put on a different persona when you write a letter? You don't need to be *you* when you do these exercises, you can be anyone you like. Part of the fun of creative writing is becoming another person, just for a little while.

Letter 5: I object!

Your local paper has published a story about a new block of flats being built on a piece of land near your house. The land is unused and covered in brambles and a couple of ancient trees.

When you were little, you used to play there when it was a tiny park, with a bench and some flower beds as well as the trees. Over time it has been left to its own devices and now the only ones playing there are the mice and birds who have made it their home.

Write to the paper, telling them why the land shouldn't be used for flats. The plans haven't gone through yet, so there is still time. Explain how you feel and give them reasons why the land should be restored or left as it is.

Here is my objection:

Dear Sir,

This land may look like it needs developing, especially as it's been left to get so messy, but let me tell you how it used to be.

It was once a lovely little park, with freshly mowed grass and flowers planted. The trees were trimmed and there was a bench for people to sit and have their lunches.

Why should it be used for yet more new builds when there are empty buildings in the middle of town? I'm sure more local people would rather have another green area for everyone than another set of flats for just a few.

Letter 6: No money!

You have been invited to attend the 21st birthday party of your youngest niece. The invitation gives the usual details as well as a note at the bottom asking for money to be given as a present because your niece wants to put it towards a new car.

You can't get out of going to the party but you really object to giving her money. You gave her money when she was 16, then again at 18 and now they want it again at 21! Your niece has been working since she was 17 and is capable of buying her own car.

Write a letter to your brother, explaining why you won't be giving any money but will be coming to the party. The tone of this letter can be anything you like.

My excuse:

Dear Tony,

You know I love Gemma like she was my own but mate, I just can't be doing with all this money giving any more. Frankly, I could do with some money giving of my own. Maybe I should have a party and invite all of you so you can pay towards a new car? Or just pay to keep the old one going through its next MOT?

So, I will be coming, as you put on a good spread and I can't afford much food these days, and I will get Gemma a nice card and say Happy Birthday, but I'm sorry, I will not be giving her any money.

And if I was you, I'd be dropping hints about her leaving home by now as well.

Letter 7: When I was young

For this letter, I need you to imagine yourself at the age of 80. You're settling down to write a letter to your great-grandson. He has just started at his new school and isn't very happy.

Write a letter telling him about when you were very small. Include any details you like, the main thing is to write it from the viewpoint of old age, so that someone very much younger can understand it and appreciate what you're telling them.

Here is my letter:

Dear Ben,

I hear you started at your new school last week? I hope you're enjoying it more by now.

When I was your age, no one minded whether I liked school or not. Aren't you lucky to have a Mummy who wants you to like school? And I bet your teachers want you to enjoy it as well.

I used to walk to school by myself, then when I was a bit older I had to take my brother in and make sure he was all right. Can you imagine when you're bigger and you can look after Millie at school?

I had to wear shorts all year round at school, no matter how cold it was. Your Mummy tells me you got a brand new uniform and it's red. That sounds great. My uniform was all grey so not half as nice as yours.

I'm looking forward to seeing you soon and hearing all about school. I've found a few photos of myself when I was your age so I'm keeping them out to show you and you can see what I looked like in my uniform.

Don't forget to do lots of things at school so you can tell me about them when I see you.

You see how this letter is longer than the others? Sometimes you need to write more, to include different angles. With this one, it was alternating between the 80 year old talking about themselves, then asking about the little grandson. When writing letters you often have to make it seem like a conversation, so that the other person feels included, especially if it is a letter to friends or family.

Letter 8: Woof!

Now for something different. You are the family dog and have just come back from kennels. Writing in any style you like, with proper sentences or simple words (eg Rufus love kennel food!), write a letter from the dog's point of view, saying what you thought of the kennels.

As this is a more difficult piece of writing, I have included two very short examples.

Simple: *Rufus come again. Want other kennel. Want one with Sindy in it.*

Complex: *I will visit you again, the next time I am free. I am very much in favour of your food and I appreciated the daily walks by the canal. Give Sindy my love.*

Letter 9: On the nose

You need to write a letter to your rich Uncle Arthur, explaining why he should lend or give you the money for a nose job.

Try to sound as if you won't be grateful for the money but still expect to get it.

Here is my begging letter:

I know you want me to be happy and I've thought long and hard about how I can be happy, so I've decided I should have a nose job.

You know what my nose looks like and you can imagine why it makes me fed up to have it on my face every day. I would visit you more often if I was happier so it would do us both good if you could pay a bit towards the cost.

Also, if it's okay with you, could you pay all of it up front, as I don't have much money at the moment. I'll pay you back when I can, probably next month. Or starting next month anyway.

Shall I call round next week to collect the money?

Letter 10: It's not me, it's you

And to finish, you are going to write a letter to the person you just met on an online dating site. You have been out for one date and you need to explain to them why you can't meet again. Use any reason you like.

My letter:

I really enjoyed meeting you the other day but I'm afraid I lied when I said I would call you and we'd get together soon. The truth is, I'm a deeply shallow person who cares about things like personal hygiene, especially at the dinner table. I just can't see a future for myself with someone who does that with a napkin. Also, for your own good I feel I should mention that there are products available that could help with your ears.

All the best and good luck in finding someone less picky or more accepting of other people's little ways.

Real Life

This section is based around real events in your own life. By learning how to describe things you have actually experienced, it then becomes easier to write about things you make up, whether they are stories or writing you need to do for work etc.

Right here, right now

To begin with, I want you to describe where you are right now. Look around you and take in all the details. You need to include things which build a picture for the reader - don't forget, they are not with you and need everything explained to them.

Here is my here and now:

I sit in a quiet room, two sofas, one for me and one for the dogs. A cat meows to get in at the window, his face full of indignation as I carry on typing.

The sun comes in through the windows and I can hear birds outside. Beside me is an empty cup of tea, waiting to be refilled.

You notice how I didn't fill the piece with details about the room but instead concentrated on creating atmosphere? A few details and some background atmosphere is sometimes better than having lots of descriptive details on their own.

Where I was

Now I want you to describe somewhere from your past. It can be from years ago or yesterday. The main thing is to explain, in words, how the place made you *feel*. So this time, the details are there to support the way you felt, as a person. Anything you include should help the reader understand your feelings, while setting the scene of the place you were in at the time.

Here is my yesterday:

I wanted so desperately to be at home. I had come out, with my little boy in tow, to show support for my husband as he visited a group of people he knew.

They were all strangers to me and as soon as I arrived, my husband left me alone and went out with them. I was left, a painfully shy young mother, with the two people still in the house. None of us knew what to say and they weren't very child-friendly, so my son didn't help with the conversation.

In the end, I could have sat and cried, but all I did instead was sit and suffer. I had gone there to be a good wife and came away vowing never to put myself through anything like that again.

You see how my feelings lead the whole piece? It can be really good writing practice to talk about how you feel, but sometimes it also means putting aside the need to keep things private.

Even if you write for yourself and no one else, it can feel like you are opening up your feelings to the whole world when you write them down. But, by doing this, you learn how to express yourself and also become less self-conscious about your writing, so do try it.

Someone close

This one is all about someone you know well. It doesn't matter who and it can be a person from many years ago or someone you see every day.

Choose someone you know well enough to describe easily. It also helps if you know how they might feel about things.

For this exercise, you are going to pretend the person you know is a character in a story. So, rather than just describing them, talk about them as if they are part of your story. For instance, don't say, 'Derek was my uncle and he was 52'; instead say, 'At the age of 52, Derek changed his life.' Do you see how a different kind of approach can alter the whole style?

It doesn't matter what you write about the person as long as you describe them well and make them seem a central part of your story.

Here is my character:

My Aunty Sarah was desperate to lose weight. She joked she wanted to live in a cage and be fed through the bars so that she couldn't over-eat anymore.

For weeks between her visits I would plan where we could put her cage and make up diet plans so that I could buy the right food.

Then Sarah would visit and laugh when I talked about the cage. She ate biscuits and cake and drank tea and did all the things she said she didn't want to do and would never tell me when we were getting the cage.

As her dresses grew tighter, she talked more about the cage but it never appeared. Somehow, I think my Aunty Sarah was never serious about losing weight.

You see how this piece of writing is about me as well as Sarah? By describing my part in her story, I help the reader understand Sarah more too. We can see how her jokes about the cage were taken seriously by little me, but that there was some truth in her saying that without the cage she would never lose weight.

Ahead of me

This time, your real-life self will have to imagine the future and decide what will happen next.

Rather than being based on a solid experience, this exercise is all about what you *hope* for in the future. It obviously hasn't happened yet but you know yourself and you know what you want and hope for, so you have to build a scenario around that.

Choose something you want for the future and work it into a piece of writing. It can be a simple descriptive passage but make it personal to you.

Here is my future:

Readers, I want to be snowed in. I want to live at the end of the track, in a beaten up house with a wild garden. I want to know that I have to shop in bulk, in case I get cut off. And I want to be able to see all visitors coming a mile away so that I can hide behind the sofa when they get here.

Finally, I want smoke rising out of a little chimney and sailing away across fields and hills, with a chill in the air and my breath floating behind it.

When people tell you the rules of how to write, they may say you shouldn't directly address your reader, as I have here. I believe that there are many ways to express ourselves and also many ways to communicate in words. I like to speak directly to my readers sometimes because I feel it bridges the gap between writer and reader.

Don't be afraid to do your own thing as you're becoming more used to writing. Just because other people don't do it, doesn't mean it can't work for you. And if it doesn't work? Well, do something else the next time. Learning to express yourself in written words is all about trying things on to see what will fit. It's a process that changes as we go along.

A new start

Think of a time when you needed to do something new. It can be a small new start or a massive one that was life changing. You could even write about both, to see the contrast.

Once you have your life event in mind, twist it around a little because I also want you to write about yourself as if you are a character in a story.

Instead of saying, 'I did' and 'I went', you are going to talk about yourself as if you are someone else.

Read my example and see what I mean:

Amanda didn't know where to look as she stood in front of the class, listening to the teacher introduce her.

A new house and now a new school. Her old school had been terrible, an awful place where she was bullied and alone. Would this be any different?

Miss Walker pointed to two girls sitting together at the other side of the room.

"Go and sit between Gail and Diane, they'll look after you today."

She went over, worried already. She was being put between two friends, would they be angry at having to look after her and not being able to sit together?

She dared to look at them and they both smiled, instantly and reassuringly. Amanda braved a smile back and Diane patted the seat she had pulled up between them.

She knew then it was going to be all right.

Do you see how you can turn your real-life experiences around and make them sound like a story? When you have experienced something, you know the details and can add things which help explain how you felt.

By talking about yourself as if you are a character in a story, you free up your descriptions in a new way. You don't have to explain yourself in the same way, you can simplify how your character feels, while still making your reader sympathise with them.

Being emotional

It can be hard to write about emotions, either your own or other people's. Even if you make up a character and know how you want them to feel, it can be difficult to work out how to describe their feelings.

For this exercise, I want you to choose an emotion and find different ways to describe it in your writing. You should choose a real-life experience, your own or someone else's. It doesn't matter which experience it is or whether you know all the facts; you need to concentrate on describing the emotions as well as you can.

Here is my emotional outburst.

I couldn't believe it! One more thing to cope with on top of everything else. I felt so upset, I didn't know what to do first. Cry, scream, shout, just rage in anger, but not really anger, more a fury of tears waiting to happen.

There was no one to make it better and then, just at that moment, the temper took over from the tears and I rushed into the kitchen and grabbed the first thing I could get my hands on.

Holding up the plate, I screamed,

"This is what I think of it all!"

As I said 'all', I flung the plate on the floor, as hard as I could. It hit the ground and I gritted my teeth together in a satisfied growl, watching it smash into pieces away from me.

You see it doesn't have to be a long piece of writing, you just need a clear description of the emotions. As you see, for this one I started off feeling upset then became angry later. In real life, our emotions are often confused or blended round the edges, so when you write about them, don't be afraid to change how you or your character feels, as this is closer to true experience than having someone with a simple, logical set of emotions.

What? What did you say?

This time we're going to be all confused in some way. You can base it on your own life, or take artistic license and stretch a real-life experience to seem more confusing.

Choose a time when you wondered what was going on, or you knew what was going on but no one else seemed to have a clue!

Describe it in any way you like, either in the first person or with yourself as a character. The idea here is to properly explain the confusion and its effect.

Here is my confused state:

Geography was one of my worst subjects, not least because the teacher seemed to take an instant dislike to me. It was a south-facing classroom and I often found myself zoning off, relaxed in the soft sunlight and almost falling asleep.

One day she was telling us about our homework. It was all about barley. That sounded as exciting as usual. I dutifully wrote down everything she said and escaped.

That night I took out the encyclopaedia and read up on barley. It was not fun but there wasn't too much to know, so I re-wrote it in my own words, decorated it with a picture of barley growing in a field and took it in.

The next lesson she was infuriated. She waved my paper at me, in front of the class and cried,

"Bali not barley! B-A-L-I! Why would we be writing about barley in geography?"

I was even more confused then as barley seemed quite close to geography, seeing as it grew in the ground in many different countries but I took back the homework without saying anything, wondering why she couldn't have spelled it the first time.

Neighbours

This is one we have all had to deal with, one way or another. Good or bad, we've all had neighbours at some point in our lives and probably also had an opinion on them.

Choose an experience which illustrates the relationship you had or have with your neighbours. You want to describe an experience which shows how you felt about each other or was a good example of what it was like to live near them.

Also, for this exercise, write the experience in the form of a letter. This means you should word it as a letter, as if you are talking to someone on paper, rather than just writing a descriptive passage.

Here is my rant:

Okay, you wouldn't believe what happened this time.

Friday night and their mother goes off on the motorbike with her boyfriend, carefree and relaxed, leaving the two daughters alone.

Then the 16 year old also goes off with her boyfriend, leaving the 13 year old to throw a brilliant party, the kind where your friends invite lots of people you don't know and bring barrels of booze.

It went on until 3am, including screaming in the street and attempts to set fire to their back garden. Then they all had a nap until 7am and were up and out, drinking on the back step. And there I was, getting up for work at 7.30 and wondering how I was going to put one leg past the other!

They had another rest, then the party re-started Saturday afternoon at 5.30, with food being thrown at the side of my house and threats to set fire to my shed. Poor Tess ambled round with half a loaf and wasn't too happy when I took it off her.

At this point, as a last resort before calling the police, I called their relatives and an irate aunt and uncle turned up to drag the house back to civilisation.

Sometimes, it would be just so nice to live next door to bears or wolves instead of people. Although, then they'd probably hunt me instead of annoying me, so maybe not.

Time to go

Let's have some nostalgia. I want you to write about your memories of the last time you were in a special place. Include details of how you felt, why it was special and if you knew it was the last time you would be there.

This exercise is in two parts, so try not to make your piece of writing too long as you'll be re-doing it later.

Here is my special goodbye:

It was the last time before we handed over the keys. After this day, the door would close and, in time, be reopened for a new family to live here.

This had been my grandparents' house for decades, my home as well for a few years and a place so imbued with memories, I could see and hear them all.

One last time I looked behind me, trying to memorise things that were already part of me and then left, softly closing the door.

Now, look again at your writing. You are going to re-write this piece, from the viewpoint of a fictional character. You'll need to change a few things so that it isn't in the first person anymore. I also want you to add a particular memory of the place, one you didn't include before.

Don't worry if this sounds a bit difficult. Use my example to help you. And don't cheat by writing it from your character's point of view first!

My goodbye part 2:

Jenna looked around the living room, thinking of all the times her grandfather had sat here, in happy solitude, watching the TV without having to be sociable with his visitors. Or peeking through the blinds, keeping an eye on all the neighbours. He worked out everyone's routines from this room.

It was the last time before Jenna had to hand over the keys. After this day, the door would close and, in time, be reopened for a new family to live here.

This had been her grandparents' house for decades; her home as well for a few years and a place so imbued with memories, she could see and hear them all.

One last time she looked behind her, trying to memorise things that were already part of her and then left, softly closing the door.

Do you see how the extra paragraph adds a different element to the story? It rounds it out more and makes it seem like a fuller story.

By writing it as yourself first, then rewriting as a character, you are becoming used to using your own memories in other kinds of written work. You don't always need to be writing about yourself to use details from your past.

This kind of thinking, separating yourself a little from something very personal, is also very useful when you come to write about yourself for more official reasons, like a job application.

It can be difficult to talk about your experience or to sell yourself but if you get more used to separating the real you from the you on the paper, then you should find it easier to talk about yourself more fully.

First impressions

Another two part exercise. The first part should be quite simple for you now that you have completed the ones before it (you *have* completed them, haven't you?)

Write about the first time you met someone who you came to know well later. This could be a friend, partner, someone you worked with; anyone you remember meeting and who gave a particular first impression. Was this impression correct or did you have them all wrong? Include this information in your writing too.

Here is my first impression:

When I met my friend Joanne, we had both just started college. She was laughing when I first caught sight of her, blonde hair bobbing as she angled her head to laugh again.

She seemed nice but not an obvious friend for me. She looked very confident and had people milling around. What would she want with a painfully shy introvert like me? And my hair never bobbed like that in its life.

It turned out she was everything I expected and yet her vivacious and relaxed personality were a very good fit for my nervous wallflower.

When we were together we had a meeting of minds and lots of laughter. I never let go of that first impression, because it had been the right one, but I learned not to make decisions on people so quickly.

For the second part of this exercise, you are going to write the first impression someone would have of *you*. This can be harder than talking about someone else but try to put yourself in another person's shoes.

You don't have to describe a time from your real life (unless this helps). Just decide what an unknown person would think when they first meet you.

Here is my own impression:

At first sight she looks like she wouldn't say boo to a goose, she seems quiet and wants to be in the background. Then I see her smiling, when she thinks no one is looking. Is she listening in to that conversation? Are people really that nosey?

Now she's watching the people over in the corner. She can't hear them from here, but she's definitely being nosey again.

I hope she doesn't take any notice of me!

Picture it

For this section we're going to use pictures to create new stories. By basing your writing on something you can see, it becomes easier to think of new ideas to match the picture.

The exercises in this section are more creative and based less on what you know, but don't be put off. No one is going to see your work and it is all just to help you practice working with new ideas.

If you have trouble thinking of what to write, try making notes based simply on the picture and the details you can draw from it. Build up to writing sentences and then move onto the story once you are ready.

What do you see?

This is the picture you come across while sorting through some old family photographs. You have never seen it before. Write a story based around the picture.

I can't remember

Write a story based on this picture and the subject of memory. It can be about losing something, forgetting something important, a memory from long ago or even making a memory in the present that will become precious in the future.

That was when...

You are writing in your diary or reading an entry from the past. Using this picture, write the diary entry, deciding what happened and what you wanted to remember in the future.

Don't forget to change your sentences to make it sound more like a diary entry, either by making them shorter or leave them as normal but styled as if you are writing to yourself.

Typical!

You've spent a lot of time organising a day out for a local group to an animal attraction 50 miles away.

It all went wrong in so many ways and now you have to write an article for your local paper, talking about the trip.

Decide whether to be honest for the article or if you are going to cover up the mishaps and make it sound positive.

Babysitting

Your sister and her husband have gone on a second honeymoon, leaving you with their children. The trouble is, the children all hate you and you're not feeling very kindly towards them.

Write an email to your sister, telling her how well you are all getting along. Make it sound positive but try to include clues as to the real situation.

This one may be a little complicated so don't be afraid to have more than one attempt. It can be a good idea to write the email as completely happy, with no problems or clues in it, then go back through it and change little things to make it more realistic.

For example, your first attempt might read:

Johnny was really proud of taking the dog for a walk today.

You could then change it to:

Johnny was really proud when he was walking the dog today, for the few minutes he held the lead.

You see how the subtle change suggests he let go of the lead, without you actually stating he did. You can imagine what happened once he let go!

Now write another email, this time to your best friend. Tell them all about your escapades with the children, including the events in the email to your sister, but this time as the unvarnished truth.

Compare how the two versions look and see how the same events can be described in different ways to create a whole new feeling within your writing.

A whole day?!

Choose an animal, anything you like as long as it's small enough to fit in your car. Now, write about what happens when you spend a day with that animal in your car. What could you do? What might go wrong? Would there be anything good about it?

Use your imagination for this one and don't be afraid to make it funny or unrealistic.

What's the worst that could happen...

What is the worst thing that could happen at work?

Write a story about things going very wrong at work but add the extra element of everyone knowing about it. This can happen right at the start or write it so that they all find out at the end.

The main thing here is to describe something unusually embarrassing or difficult. Don't stick with the ordinary, make it as bad as it can be.

Getting away from it all

You've won an all-expenses paid trip to a charming country cottage in the middle of a forest, miles from anyone or anything.

When you get there, it isn't quite what you expected but by then the taxi has left and you have no choice but to make the best of it.

Using the picture, write a story based on your experiences in the cottage. You can decide on the theme, so choose whether it will be a horror, thriller, comedy, romance or anything else you like.

Toby Tickle-Toes

Looking after someone else's pet is never easy but when he is a spoiled rodent called Toby Tickle-Toes, it gets even harder.

Write a short story about what happens when you look after your friend's pet mouse, hamster, guinea pig, gerbil or rat. Include plenty of descriptive words, including what Toby looks like and how you feel about him.

Now, re-write what you have written in shorter, more simple and direct sentences. You want it to sound more like a children's story, the kind you would have in a picture book.

This can be harder than you would think as you need to make it exciting and descriptive without going into too much detail.

Nowhere to turn

For this exercise, you are going to write about a nightmare. Base it on the picture and make it one of those times when you can't wake from a dream.

Write anything you like as there are no limits in dreams, but when you reach the end of the story, include an unexpected twist.

An ending

Here we are, at the end of our writing. Do you remember the exercise you did at the very beginning, where you introduced yourself? Well, I want you to do that one again.

Don't read your old attempt, not yet. Just write about yourself, including as much detail as possible. What makes you interesting? What sets you apart? What would you like other people to know?

Once you have finished (properly finished, no rushing!), go back to your original work and compare it with this one.

Can you see changes in the way you have written about yourself? Have you written more or included different details? Do you sound like the same person?

Hopefully, you now see your writing in a different light but don't let your journey stop here. There are so many ways to express yourself and writing is just one of them. Always try new ways of writing and don't be afraid to experiment with how you do things.

The more practice you give yourself, the more confidence you will have and the better you will express your thoughts and feelings in the written word.

For more details of my books and free resources, visit
www.thewishatree.com

26206416R00034

Printed in Poland
by Amazon Fulfillment
Poland Sp. z o.o., Wrocław